T0403199

On Vacation

LEVEL 7

/o/

Teaching Tips

Turquoise Level 7

This book focuses on the grapheme **/o/**.

Before Reading

- Discuss the title. Ask readers what they think the book will be about. Have them support their answer.
- Ask readers to sort the words on page 3. Read the words together. Reinforce that /o/ can have a short /o/ sound or a long /o/ sound.

Read the Book

- Encourage readers to read independently, either aloud or silently to themselves.
- Prompt readers to break down unfamiliar words into units of sound and string the sounds together to form the words. Then, ask them to look for context clues to see if they can figure out what these words mean. Discuss new vocabulary to confirm meaning.
- Urge readers to point out when the focused phonics grapheme appears in the text. Does it have a short /o/ sound or a long /o/ sound?

After Reading

- Ask readers comprehension questions about the book. Where did people in the book go on vacation? Where would you like to go?
- Encourage readers to think of other words with the /o/ grapheme. On a separate sheet of paper, have them write the words in two columns: one for the short /o/ sound and the other for the long /o/ sound.

© 2024 Booklife Publishing
This edition is published by arrangement with Booklife Publishing.

North American adaptations © 2024 Jump!
5357 Penn Avenue South
Minneapolis, MN 55419
www.jumplibrary.com

Library of Congress Cataloging-in-Publication Data is available at www.loc.gov or upon request from the publisher.

ISBN: 979-8-88524-775-7 (hardcover)
ISBN: 979-8-88524-776-4 (paperback)
ISBN: 979-8-88524-777-1 (ebook)

Photo Credits

Images are courtesy of Shutterstock.com. With thanks to Getty Images, Thinkstock Photo and iStockphoto. Cover – GOLFX, Iakov Kalinin, ayelet-keshet. p4–5 – Niyazz, Angelo Giampiccolo. p6–7 – Ana Flasker, cktravels.com. p8–9 – Wirestock Creators, Dirk M. de Boer, COULANGES. p10–11 – BlueOrange Studio, Wasim Khuzam. p12–13 – gorillaimages, FooTToo. p14–15 – Odua Images, Monkey Business Images. p16 – Shutterstock.

Can you sort these words into two groups? One group has o as in **fold**. One group has o as in **hot**.

Bolt

Not

Crop

Cold

Stop

Block

Molt

Have you ever been on a vacation? We will go on vacation in this book. We can go to lots of different parts of the planet!

People get around the planet on planes.
The pilot sits in the front of the plane. It is
called the cockpit. It has lots of controls.

It is hot in Morocco. You can feel the heat when the plane door opens. In Morocco, you can go to the beach and in the sea.

Morocco

You can go to markets in Morocco. You can meet local sellers who will sell you gifts for money. You might get a shirt or a toy.

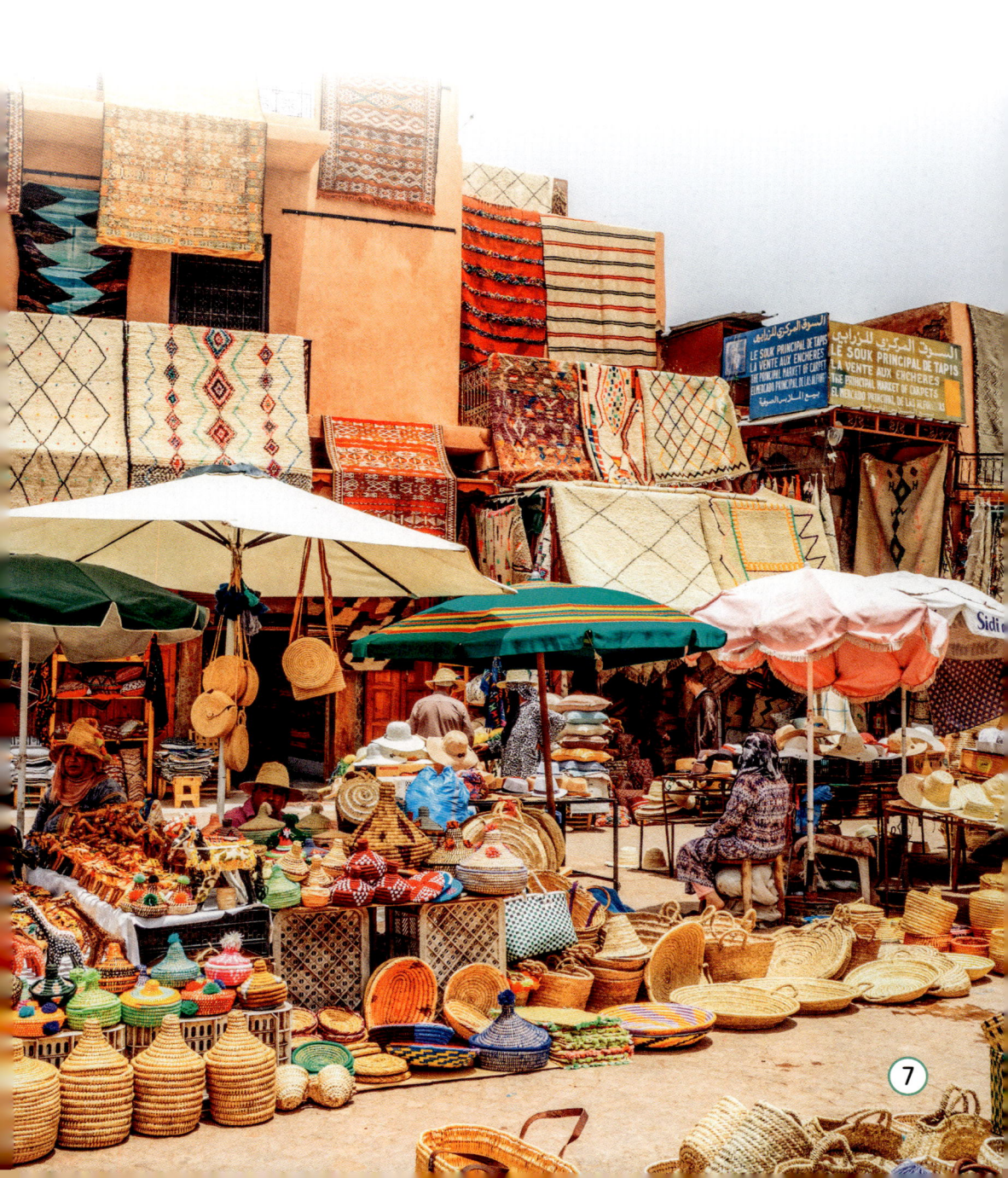

It is time to go on to the next part of the planet! In Brazil, you can find the Amazon rain forest and the Amazon River. You can see lots of animals.

You can see monkeys in the trees. They swing from tree to tree. You can see dolphins in the Amazon River too. They have a pink color.

Now we can go to a cold part of the planet.
Put on a scarf and a coat if you go to Finland.

Forest in Finland

In Finland, you might go in a hot sauna to get out of the cold. Finland has a lot of good spots for a photo.

On to another cold part of the planet! People go to the Alps to ski. They ski down the hills. Could you ski like a pro?

Lots of people also stay in log cabins among the hills. A log cabin can be a home for when you are away.

You do not have to travel far to go on vacation.
It can be a lot of fun to stay near home.

Pack up the car!

I wonder which part of the planet you will go to. Whether it is hot or cold, have the best time ever on vacation!

Say the name of each object below. Is the "o" in each a short /o/ or a long /o/ sound?

yogurt

piano

dog

mop